Survival Family Basics

The Prepper's Emergency First Aid and Survival Medicine Handbook

Macenzie Guiver

Macenzie Guiver

© 2014

All Rights Reserved. **No part of this publication may be reproduced in any form or by any means, including scanning, photocopying, or otherwise without prior written permission of the copyright holder.**

Disclaimer and Terms of Use: The Author and Publisher have strived to be as accurate and complete as possible in the creation of this book, notwithstanding the fact that he does not warrant or represent at any time that the contents within are accurate due to the rapidly changing nature of the Internet. While all attempts have been made to verify information provided in this publication, the Author and Publisher assume no responsibility for errors, omissions, or contrary interpretation of the subject matter herein. Any perceived slights of specific persons, peoples, or organizations are unintentional. In practical advice books, like anything else in life, there are no guarantees of income made or health benefits received. This book is not intended for use as a source of medical, legal, business, accounting or financial advice. All readers are advised to seek services of competent professionals in medical, legal, business, accounting, and finance matters.

Printed in the United States of America

Survival Family Basics

Just to say Thank You for Purchasing this Book I want to give you a gift 100% absolutely FREE

A Copy of My Upcoming Special Report "*The Prepper's Supplies Guide for When Disaster Strikes*"

Go to www.SurvivalFamilyBasics.com to Sign Up to Receive Your FREE Gift

Table of Content

INTRODUCTION	6
THE IMPORTANCE OF PREPAREDNESS	8
PREPARE FOR YOUR LIFESTYLE!	9
TYPES OF DISASTERS AND POTENTIAL INJURIES	11
NATURAL DISASTERS	11
Potential Damage and Injuries from Natural Disasters	*12*
MAN-MADE DISASTERS	13
Potential Damage and Injuries from Man-made Disasters	*13*
THE DIFFERENCE BETWEEN EMERGENCY FIRST AID AND SURVIVAL MEDICINE	14
EMERGENCY FIRST AID	14
SURVIVAL MEDICINE	15
YOUR EMERGENCY FIRST AID KIT	16
PREPPING YOUR KIT SHOULD NOT BE CHALLENGING!	16
First Aid Kit Standard Contents	*17*
Unconventional Items	*18*
Specific for Your Family	*18*
SURVIVAL MEDICATIONS	20
Over the Counter (OTC) Medications to be Included in Your Kit	*20*
Prescription Medications for Your Kit	*21*
Alternative Medicines	*21*
BASIC FIRST AID	23
REMEMBER THERE IS NO CPR IN FIRST AID	23
HEAD TO TOE ASSESSMENT	24
ABC's	*25*
Look for Injuries	*25*
Communicate with the Victim	*27*
Closed-Head, Neck, and Spinal Injuries	*27*
Items to stabilize the spine:	*29*
Items that may be used to stabilize the head and neck:	*30*

TREATING INJURIES	**31**
BURNS	31
Classification of Burns	*32*
Dos and Don'ts of Burn Treatment	*33*
General Guidelines for Treating Chemical and Inhalation Burns	*34*
WOUND CARE	37
Control Bleeding	*37*
Clean the Wound	*37*
Apply Dressings and Bandages	*38*
Rules for Dressing Wounds	*38*
Impaled Objects	*38*
TREATING FRACTURES, DISLOCATIONS, SPRAINS, AND STRAINS	40
Fractures	*40*
Dislocations	*43*
Sprains and Strains	*43*
Splinting	*44*
NASAL INJURIES	46
BITES AND STINGS	47
Allergic Reactions & Anaphylaxis	*48*
TREATING COLD-RELATED INJURIES	49
Hypothermia	*49*
Frostbite	*51*
TREATING HEAT-RELATED INJURIES	52
Heat cramps	*52*
Heat Exhaustion	*52*
Heat Stroke	*53*
HANDLING THE DEAD	**54**
CONCLUSION	**57**
CHECK OUT THESE OTHER *SURVIVAL FAMILY BASICS* TITLES…	**57**
REFERENCES	**61**

Introduction

I want to thank you and congratulate you for downloading the book, "*Survival Family Basics - The Prepper's Emergency First Aid and Survival Medicine Handbook*".

Limiting the severity of destruction, whether from human or natural causes, begins with preparedness. This book is the first tool to place in your Prepper's Emergency First Aid and Survival Medication Kit.

This book contains proven steps and strategies, from over 25-years of Disaster Response and Emergency Preparedness, on how to build an emergency first aid kit with traditional items and non-traditional items, identify the signs and symptoms of life threatening injuries that occur during disasters, administering emergency first aid treatment, and having knowledge of essential survival medications both pharmaceutical and homeopathic.

As the roar of the destruction begins to fade in the background will you know how to provide emergency first aid to those around you?

When the public service announcement disrupts your favorite television show, will you know what do following a chemical attack?

After completing this book, you will be able to identify which injuries are most likely to occur with a disaster and how to administer basic first aid that may make the difference between life and death.

You will have an understanding of manmade terrorism events and resources to keep you and your family safe. You'll soon view the common household items in your home as rescue items and survival medications.

During a disaster, Emergency Medical Services (EMS) and hospitals are rapidly overwhelmed. We have all too frequently heard of community centers and school football fields becoming make shift triage centers and morgues.

The best way to ensure that you and your family make it out of a disaster situation with a positive outcome is to plan and Prep. That's what we're about to do, so let's get started!

Macenzie Guiver

The Importance of Preparedness

Disasters occur with little or no warning. No one likes to think about disaster striking our home and disrupting or harming our families. But disasters do occur and can impact or even devastate our lives.

The psychological damage is not often visible although the destruction of our homes and communities is. Lives are destroyed and lives must be rebuilt. It is important to think about the factors that can impact each and every one of us.

Studies have shown than preparedness has a positive impact in a crisis situation. The speed of recovery from a disaster depends on how well you have planned and prepared. You can protect your family by identifying the risks associated with natural and man-made disasters by making an emergency medicine disaster and survival kit.

Government officials recommend that you should be able to care for yourself and your family for up to 72 hours before help arrives. That may or may not be enough.

The factors involved depend on the declared disaster area, or the location where the emergency occurs and the time it takes to get resources to the affected area when the scale of a disaster is great.

Thinking and planning for a disaster can be frightening but following this guide, there are simple steps to make it easy.

Having the available resources to treat an injured person is often the biggest hurdle. Learning what type of injuries to look for following a specific emergency and thinking outside the box will simplify putting together your emergency first aid kit.

If you run into a roadblock or would like to integrate your emergency first aid and survival medicine kit into your neighborhood's plan, share the knowledge you are learning. Speak to your family, friends and local emergency planning committee. It's always best to know what resources are available.

You never know when disaster will strike, and because of that your family may not be together when it does. Having your emergency first aid and survival medicine kit prepared in advance will decrease confusion and increase the likelihood of you and your family not only surviving a disaster, but thriving.

Prepare for your lifestyle!

Ask yourself where you will keep your plan, how many emergency kits will you need.

Letting your family help you put your kit together not only provides family time but it also educates other family members on what is in the kit and how to use the items.

Start prepping as a family. Each family member should make a list of their medical concerns, and items they specifically would need. (For example, if you or your family member wears contact lenses, then have spare contact lenses, solutions, and glasses in your emergency first aid kit. Consider adding a contact lens removal syringe, and irrigation syringe for eye emergencies.) Having conversations like this will assist in prepping for your families unique needs.

List medications, physicians, and specialist and contact numbers. Always have several copies. Remember, one kit is never enough when a real disaster strikes.

Always prepare for your community and your lifestyle. If you are a family that enjoys camping and hiking. Have an emergency first aid and survival medicine kit for your camping trips. In those kits, you may consider adding additional items for bites and stings.

If you live in a rural remote area and flash flooding occurs, consider the possibility of evacuation, or car emersion. Place brightly colored bandages and dressings, and floatation devises in your go kits.

Make sure your plan and your kit fits you!

Types of Disasters and Potential Injuries

A disaster is a severe emergency that results in injury, death and destruction of property and overwhelms resources. Disasters are categorized in two ways: Natural and Man-made. Natural disasters can occur with little to no warning, although hurricanes can be predicted with time for evacuation.

Natural disasters

In the United States (including, Guam, Virgin Islands and Puerto Rico) each year out of 100,000 thunderstorms, on average 10,000 of those are severe, resulting in 5, 000 floods, 1,000 tornadoes and 2 deadly hurricanes. 90% of presidentially declared disasters are weather related with an average of over 500 deaths.

Natural disasters consist of: earthquakes, flooding (flash flooding), tornado, fires, avalanches, volcanic eruptions, winter storms, and extreme heat.

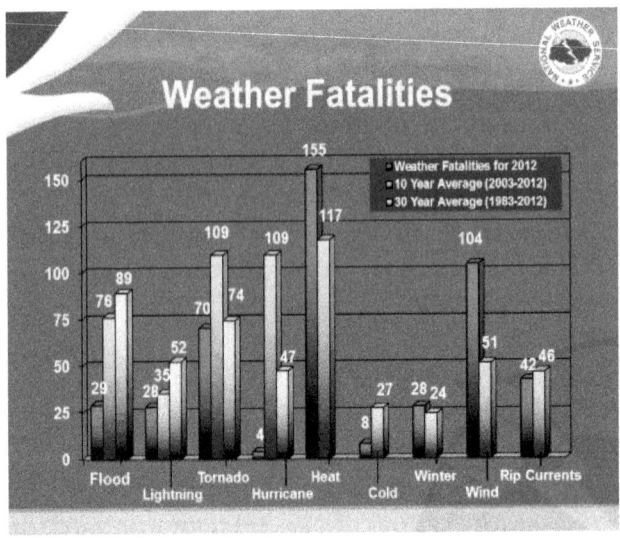

Potential Damage and Injuries from Natural Disasters

- Tornados:
  Flying debris and fallen objects (blunt force injuries, crush injuries, impaled injuries)
- Earthquakes:
  Fallen objects, broken gas lines, downed power lines (crush injuries, blast injuries, burns)
- Floods/Tsunamis:
  Carbon monoxide poisoning (dizziness, light head, nausea) drowning, electrocution from fallen power lines.
- Ice Storms:
  Hypothermia and frostbite
- Volcanic Eruptions:
  Toxic gas released, flash flooding of hot water and debris resulting in burns and eye injuries.
- Landslides:

Crush injuries, drowning (suffocation) from powerful moving water. Trauma from debris. Electrocution from broken power lines.

Man-made disasters

A man-made disaster results from hazards or threats related to human development and intent.

Potential Damage and Injuries from Man-made Disasters

- Biological Disasters:
  Anthrax, SARS; Flu like symptoms; respiratory arrest
    o Know your local plan. Many cities in the United States have a biological emergency plan supported by the federal government.
    o Listen to your television, radio or NOAA weather station. Instructions will be provided to citizens where their local mass dispensing sites are to receive antibiotics.
    o Limited medical care will be available due to surge of patients in hospitals

- Chemical Disasters:
  Seizure activity; sudden death

- Radiological/Nuclear Disasters:
  Internal and External Contamination of self and family

The Difference Between Emergency First Aid and Survival Medicine

Emergency First Aid

Emergency First Aid is often performed by a lay person prior to the victim receiving medical care by a licensed professional. There are times when first aid may be only the care required such as cleansing a cut or applying a dressing. There may also be circumstances when emergency first aid may be the difference between life and death.

Life saving techniques can be performed when administering first aid that will open an individual's airway to promote breathing. Other techniques may assist in slowing bleeding or splinting a fracture limb.

The ABC's in first aid are referred to as: Airway, Bleeding and Circulation. Often in disaster first aid, the terminology of "The 3 Killers" may be used. These are the same and identify: blocked airway, excessive bleeding and shock.

The individual providing first aid may be called "the rescuer", but it is always important to know that before you administer any treatment you must be safe yourself. The object is NOT for you to become a victim as well.

Stop, take a deep breath and look at your surroundings before providing any aid. We'll go into this more, later in the book.

Survival Medicine

Survival medicine is a practice of medicine in an environment where standard medical care facilities are unavailable and is performed by an individual with no formal training.

In an emergency situation, with limited or no resources available, informal medical care is generally better than *no* medical care.

Often using unconventional items and techniques is the only way to relieve pain, decrease the damage from injury, reduce suffering, or even be the difference between life and death.

Your Emergency First Aid Kit

A well- stocked first aid kit is a must. It should be assembled ahead of time and be ready for anything; adapted to your life style and placed in your safe room of your home.

Never remove items just because you can't find something around your home for a non- emergency. Using your Emergency Kit scissors to wrap a birthday gift, while tempting, could cost your family dearly in a disaster, just don't do it!

Prepping your kit should not be challenging!

Your kit does not have to be the standard small box or official First Aid bag. Always think outside of the box. A plastic tote, old suitcase or duffel bag are quite practical and provide the space for sterile water, splinting products, and everything else you'll need.

Add go kits to your car, work place, vacation home, and your garage.

Survival Family Basics

All emergency first aid kits should be assembled with basic items.

Be creative. After you have completed this chapter, walk through your home and identify items that you already have to build a basic kit – there's no need to go out and spend a small fortune here.

Once your kit is complete with the basic items, write the date on your calendar that you assembled it, then check every three months for expired items.

Always plan your first aid kit specific to your family or those within your home.
- Will you need daily medications?
- Do you wear contact lenses?
- Are you a diabetic?
- Do other members of your home have special needs?

If you have a large family, you may want to double or even triple the amount of contents.

First Aid Kit Standard Contents

- First aid manual
- Sterile adhesive bandages in assorted sizes
- Two-inch sterile gauze pads (4-6)
- Four-inch sterile gauze pads (4-6)
- Hypoallergenic adhesive tape
- Assorted sizes of safety pins
- Cleaning agent/soap/alcohol
- Non-latex exam gloves (2 pairs)
- Cotton balls
- Sunscreen
- Three-inch sterile roller bandages (3 rolls)

- Triangular bandages (3)
- Needle
- Moistened towelettes
- Antibacterial ointment
- Thermometer
- Tongue depressor (2)
- Tube of petroleum jelly or other lubricant
- Four-inch sterile roller bandages (3 rolls)
- Scissors
- Tweezers
- Hot and cold compress
- Trash Bags (for debris as well as cover during rain)

Unconventional Items

- Panty hose for immobilizing broken limbs
- Duct Tape (securing broken limbs, marking the dead)
- Dried beans (place in panty hose and used to secure the head and neck)
- Plastic siding (Various sizes) for splinting limbs or molded to collect water
- Tea bags (for clotting missing teeth)
- Reusable Plastic Bags
- Paper and permanent marker
- Bed Sheet (to secure broken limbs when splinting or to cover the deceased)

Specific for Your Family

For Infants
- Diapers
- Trash bags and Ties (for soiled clothing and diapers)
- Teething gel
- Baby Wash

For the Elderly
- Peri Wash
- Denture Adhesive
- Prescription medications
- Additional Water (denture cleanser, for medications, additional hydration needs)
- Body lotion
- Heat packs (Elderly are susceptible to hypothermia)

For Diabetics
- Glucose Tabs
- Glucometer and supplies
- Peanut Butter (for hypoglycemia)
- Graham Crackers
- Additional Bandages and dressings (Diabetics are more susceptible to skin breakdown and skin infections)

Survival Medications

Survival Medications are the "must have" medications for survival and the basic medicines to have in an emergency first aid kit.

A purchased basic first aid kit will include over the counter medications but these are not necessarily what *your* family will need.

Don't discount the basics though. Although anti-diarrhea medications does not sound like an essential component in your survival pharmacy, if someone consumes contaminated water or spoiled food, the body will purge and dehydration is not far behind. At that time, the anti-diarrhea medication may be the difference between life and death.

Over the Counter (OTC) Medications to be Included in Your Kit

- Anti-bacterial ointment
- Allergy medication
- Activated charcoal (may need to be prescribed in some states or countries)
- Laxatives
- Peroxide
- Sterile Water
- Non aspirin pain reliever
- Glucose tablets
- Vitamins
- Cough Suppressants
- Anti-diarrheal medications
- Aspirin

Prescription Medications for Your Kit

Any prescription medications that are prescribed for you and your family by your family physician need to be in there. Quite often, if you discuss this with your personal doctor, they will assist you in your disaster planning and preparedness.

Alternative Medicines

- Raw Honey (mix with Garlic Oil or Fresh Ginger for Antibiotic effect, can also be mixed with hit water and drunk for colds – also apply to serious burns or wounds)
- Garlic oil (antibiotic properties)
- Apple Cider Vinegar (dozens of uses)
- Aloe Vera Gel (for burns)
- Cayenne Pepper (topically for joint pain relief – also has antibiotic properties)
- Eucalyptus oil (great decongestant
- Geranium Oil (decreases bleeding when applied to wounds, lowers blood sugar, antibacterial)
- Helichrysum Oil (anti-inflammatory, analgesic [pain reliever])
- Lavender Oil (antiseptic, anti-insomnia, stress relief, good for rashes and cuts)
- Peppermint oil (for headaches, a respiratory and nasal decongestant, digestive disorders including nausea)
- Tea tree essential oil (antiseptic, anti-fungal, and good for insect bites)
- Thyme oil (antispasmodic for coughs, cramps, and spasms, antibacterial, antiseptic, and can be used as insect repellant

- Chamomile tea bags (relaxing, good for headache and digestive problems, can be used as a compress for burns and insect stings)
- Echinacea tea bags (supports immune system, decreases flu and cold duration)
- Ginger tea bags- (good for nausea, stomach aches, gas and bloating, as well as motion sickness)
- Multi-vitamins
- Vitamin C
- Zinc
- Other supplements to strengthen the immune system

Basic First Aid

Basic first aid is the process of performing an assessment of the injured. This could be an individual injured during a disaster, someone who is choking, having a heart attack, allergic reaction from medications, food allergy, bite or sting.

Emergency first aid rescuers are trained in injuries such as cuts, abrasions, burns, broken bones (fractures), frost bite, and various bites and stings. Care provided is often small bandages and dressings, splinting broken bones, remove stingers, applying topical ointments, and getting a victim from an unsafe environment to a safe environment with the least amount of damage possible.

Always seek professional medical help as soon as you are able.

That said, a first aid rescuer can quite often apply care and no further treatment may be necessary.

In a normal situation where a life threatening injury is apparent, a rescuer will provide first aid and wait for the ambulance to arrive.

In a disaster event, first aid treatment can make the difference between life and death, when help may or may not be on its way.

Remember There is No CPR in First Aid

First Aid places the emphasis on how to identify if an injured individual is alert, if their airway is open, stop any bleeding and prevent shock.

Cardiopulmonary Resuscitation (CPR) is a technique to attempt to remove obstructions preventing a person from breathing, assist breathing and hands on stimulation to promote circulation of blood when the heart is not pumping.

It is important to remember when beginning CPR; one does not *stop* CPR until a licensed medical provider takes over from a lay person.

In a wide scale disaster with minimal resources available it may be hours or days before a medical professional arrives. If you as a rescuer can't stop CPR once you start, you have the weight the consequences to yourself and others. Disaster medical operation teams often stress using good judgment when making the decision to start or stop CPR.

Head to Toe Assessment

Before administering first aid, be sure you are being a *safe* rescuer.

Identify your surroundings to be sure the area is safe for you.

Wear proper attire! Always wear latex or rubber gloves to prevent fluid contamination and goggles if they are available.

Head-to-toe assessments should be verbal and hands-on. Always conduct head-to-toe assessments in the same way — beginning with the head and moving toward the feet.

If injuries to the head, neck, or spine are suspected, the main objective is to not cause additional injury.

Use in-line stabilization and a backboard if the victim must be moved (more on this later).

Survival Family Basics

ABC's

When conducting a Head-to-toe assessment you will be watching for the 3 Killers or the ABC's.
- Airway obstruction (is the tongue blocking the airway?)
- Bleeding (Excessive, pumping)
- Circulation (Signs of shock)

Look for Injuries

Systematically check the victim to identify injuries and determine what will be needed to treat him or her.

Periodically look at your hands for blood. Check the limbs, arms and legs, for pulses, see if they can move their arms and legs and can feel your touch. Always look for medical bracelets.

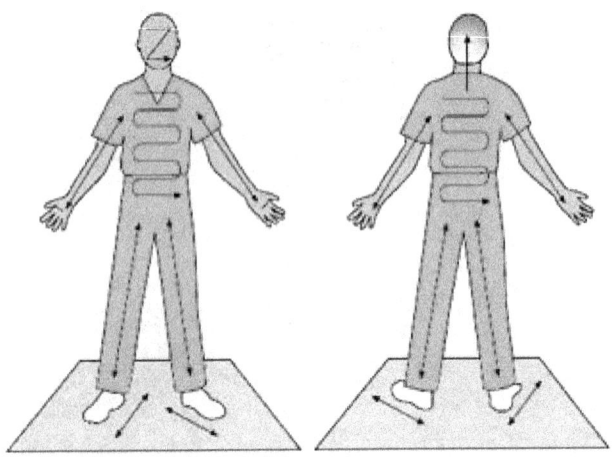

Observe the victim for the following:

- Deformities
- Contusions (bruising)
- Abrasions
- Punctures
- Burns
- Tenderness
- Lacerations
- Swelling

Carefully check the following:

- Head
- Neck
- Shoulders
- Chest
- Arms
- Abdomen
- Pelvis
- Legs

Communicate with the Victim

If the person is upset or anxious, speaking to them can help calm them down.

If you need to remove clothing always explain to the victim why this is necessary and get their permission to do so.

While conducting the assessment, pay close attention and compare each arm and   each leg to the other. If there is a change, deformity this is a sign of a broken limb,   fracture.

If they aren't speaking to you, have you identified that their airway is fully open and they are breathing.

If the patient is unconscious from trauma, be careful of movement and treat them as if the spine is injured.

Closed-Head, Neck, and Spinal Injuries

When conducting head-to-toe assessments, the injured victim may have suffered a closed head injury or spinal injury.

A closed head injury is a concussion-type injury, as opposed to a laceration, although lacerations can be an indication that the victim has also suffered a closed-head injury.

Always do everything possible to keep from moving the patient. Keep the head and neck still by having another individual hold both sides of the neck in head. Always minimize movement of the head and spine.

Signs of a Closed-Head, Neck, or Spinal Injury

The signs of a closed-head, neck, or spinal injury most often include:
- Change in consciousness
- Inability to move one or more body parts
- Severe pain or pressure in head, neck, or back
- Tingling or numbness in extremities
- Difficulty breathing or seeing
- Heavy bleeding, bruising, or deformity of the head or spine
- Blood or fluid in the nose or ears
- Bruising behind the ear
- "Raccoon" eyes (bruising around eyes)
- "Uneven" pupils
- Seizures
- Nausea or vomiting
- Victim found under collapsed building material or heavy debris

If the victim is exhibiting any of these signs, he or she should be treated as having a closed-head, neck, or spinal injury.

How to Stabilize the Head and Spine

In a disaster or emergency situation the rescuer may need to be creative and think outside of the box for equipment. There are several items that could be used to place the injured victim on. A flat, solid object will stabilize the spine and provide ease of movement of the injured victim.

Survival Family Basics

Items to stabilize the spine:
- Plywood
- Doors
- Removable table tops
- For Children, plastic or wooden sleds

The head and neck will need to be stabilized to prevent movement. The items should be tucked closely around both sides of the head to prevent movement.

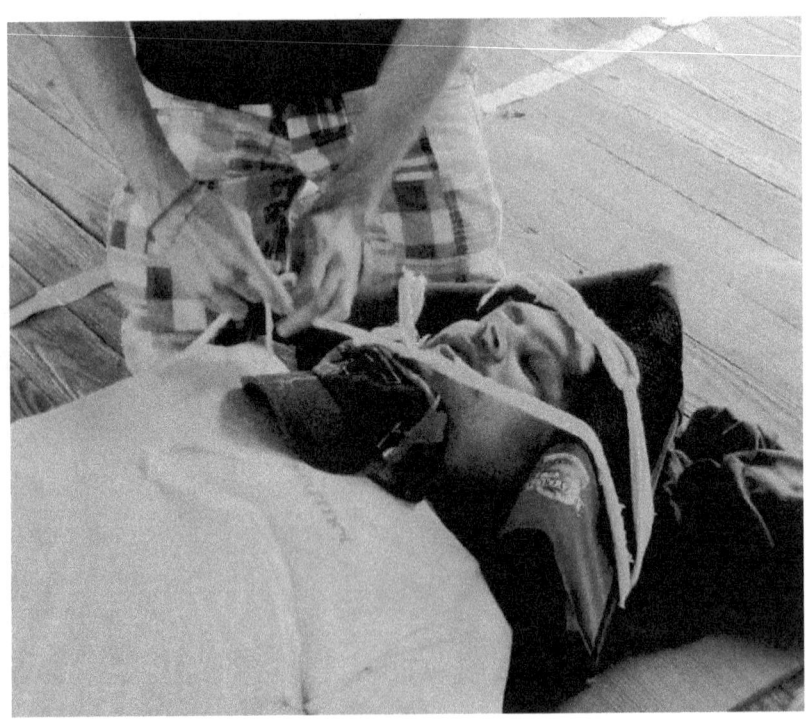

Items that may be used to stabilize the head and neck:
- Towels
- Sheets
- Clothing
- Curtains
- Panty hose filled with dried beans

Treating Injuries

Infection, cross contamination, and soiled items become public health threats in large scale disasters. In any emergency, it is always a priority to maintain proper hygiene and sanitation and purify water if necessary. Always plan and prepare to address these issues.

That said, let's dive straight in to the different types of injuries and how to deal with them.

Burns

Burns are classified as superficial, partial thickness, or full thickness depending on severity and the depth of skin layers involved.

Treatment for burns involves removing the source of the burn, cooling the burn, and covering it. For full thickness burns, always treat for shock.

The first step in treating burns is to conduct a thorough assessment.

Always ask what caused the burn, is the threat (danger) still present.

The objectives of first aid treatment for burns are to:

- Cool the burned area
- Cover with a sterile cloth to reduce the risk of infection (by keeping fluids in and germs out)

Burns may be caused by heat, chemicals, electrical current, or radiation. The severity of a burn depends on the:

- Temperature of the burning agent
- Period of time that the victim was exposed
- Area of the body that was affected
- Size of the area burned
- Depth of the burn

The skin has three layers:

- The epidermis, or outer layer of skin, contains nerve endings and is penetrated by hairs.
- The dermis, or middle layer of skin, contains blood vessels, oil glands, hair follicles, and sweat glands.
- The subcutaneous layer, or innermost layer, contains blood vessels and overlies the muscles.

Depending on the severity, burns may affect all three layers of skin.

Classification of Burns

Classification	Skin Layers Affected	Signs
Superficial	Epidermis	Reddened, dry skin Pain Swelling (possible)
Partial Thickness	Epidermis Partial destruction of dermis	Reddened, blistered skin Wet appearance Pain

		Swelling (possible)
Full Thickness	Complete destruction of epidermis and dermis Possible subcutaneous damage (destroys all layers of skin)	Whitened, leathery, or charred (brown or black) Painful or relatively painless

Dos and Don'ts of Burn Treatment

When treating a burn victim, DO:

1. Remove the victim from the burning source.
2. Put out any flames and remove smoldering clothing unless it is stuck to the skin.
3. Cool skin or clothing if they are still hot by immersing them in cool water for not more than 1 minute or covering with clean compresses that have been soaked in cool water and wrung out. Cooling sources include water from the bathroom or kitchen; garden hose; and soaked towels, sheets, or other cloths. Treat all victims of full thickness burns for shock.

4. Cover loosely with dry, sterile dressings to keep air out, reduce pain, and prevent infection.

5. Elevate above the heart to help relieve pain.

6. Infants, young children, and older persons, and persons with severe burns, are more susceptible to hypothermia. Therefore, rescuers should use caution when applying cool dressings on such persons. A rule of thumb is do not cool more than 15% of the body

surface area at a time (the size of one arm), to prevent hypothermia.

7. Wrap fingers and toes loosely and individually when treating severe burns to the hands and feet.

8. Loosen clothing near the affected area. Remove jewelry if necessary, taking care to document what was removed, when, and to whom it was given.

When treating a burn victim, DO NOT:

1. Do not use ice. Ice causes blood vessel constriction.

2. Do not apply antiseptics, ointments, or other remedies.

3. Do not remove shreds of tissue, break blisters, or remove adhered particles of clothing. (Cut burned-in clothing around the burn.)

General Guidelines for Treating Chemical and Inhalation Burns

Chemical and inhalation burns vary from traditional heat-related burns in their origin and treatment.

Guidelines for Treating Inhalation Burns

Remember that 60 to 80% of fire fatalities are the result of smoke inhalation.

Whenever fire and/or smoke are present, the rescuer should assess victims for signs and symptoms of smoke inhalation.

These are indicators that an inhalation burn is present:

- Sudden loss of consciousness
- Evidence of respiratory distress or upper airway obstruction
- Soot around the mouth or nose
- Singed facial hair
- Burns around the face or neck
- The patient may not present these signs and symptoms until hours (sometimes up to a full 24 hours) after the injury occurred, and such symptoms may be overlooked when treating more obvious signs of trauma.

Smoke inhalation is the number one cause of fire-related death.

Chemical Burns

Unlike more traditional burns, chemical burns do not result from extreme heat, and therefore treatment differs greatly. They are not always obvious.

Consider chemical burns as a possibility if the victim's skin is burning and there is no sign of a fire.

- Protect yourself from contact with the substance. Use your protective gear — especially goggles, mask, and gloves.
- *After* taking necessary actions to protect yourself, remove the clothing from the victim and place in a trash bag and seal.
- Ensure that any affected clothing or jewelry is removed from the victim.

- If the irritant is dry, gently brush away as much as possible. Always brush away from the eyes and away from the victim and you.
- Use lots of cool running water to flush the chemical from the skin for 15 minutes preferably in a shower or with a garden hose. The running water will dilute the chemical fast enough to prevent the injury from getting worse. (Be sure to contain the chemical thought and not contaminate the ground or drinking water.)
- Watch the victim for seizure activity. Monitor the victim's level of consciousness and breathing. If necessary, rescue breathing may need to be performed.

Poison Control Centers should be notified if possible in the event of a chemical burn. If the chemical burn is related to a chemical spill and the container is available, then it is possible to identify on the container how to treat the burn.

If the chemical burn is related to a terrorism event, the rescuer safety should first protect themselves. If chemical terrorism gear is available, the rescuer should take appropriate action and don the gear.

Wound Care

The main treatment for wounds includes:
- Control bleeding
- Clean the wound
- Apply dressing and bandage

Control Bleeding

Bleeding should always be controlled prior to cleansing the wound.

If the blood is bright red and pumping, this is serious and all efforts should be made to stop the bleed by applying pressure. Never remove the dressing, just apply more dressing and hold pressure. If necessary, elevate the injury above the heart.

Tourniquets are not the first line of defense to stop bleeding. Always keep in mind that the injured is at high risk to lose the limb when a tourniquet is applied because of blood flow restriction. In a situation where all other efforts to stop the bleeding have failed then, and only then apply a tourniquet. Mark the time it was applied and check for a pulse and coolness of the extremity periodically.

Clean the Wound

Wounds should be cleaned by irrigating with clean, room temperature water.

NEVER use hydrogen peroxide to irrigate the wound.

You should not scrub the wound, rather use a bulb syringe for irrigation. In a disaster, a turkey baster may also be useful.

Apply Dressings and Bandages

When the wound is thoroughly cleaned, you will need to apply a dressing and bandage to help keep it clean and maintain control of bleeding.

There is a difference between a dressing and a bandage:
- A dressing is applied directly to the wound. Whenever possible, a dressing should be sterile.
- A bandage holds the dressing in place.

If a wound is still bleeding, the bandage should place enough pressure on the wound to help control bleeding without interfering with circulation unless it is pumping blood as mention above.

Rules for Dressing Wounds

You should follow these rules for dressing wounds:
- If there is active bleeding (i.e., if the dressing is soaked with blood), redress over the existing dressing and maintain pressure and elevation to control bleeding.
- In the absence of active bleeding, remove the dressings, flush the wound, and then check for signs of infection at least every 4 to 6 hours.

Impaled Objects

Sometimes, you may also encounter a victim with a foreign object lodged in their body — usually as the result of flying debris during the disaster.

When a foreign object is impaled in a patient's body, you should:

- Immobilize the affected body part
- Do Not attempt to move or remove the object, unless it is obstructing the airway.
- Try to control bleeding at the entrance wound without placing undue pressure on the foreign object
- Clean and dress the wound making sure to stabilize the impaled object. Wrap bulky dressings around the object to keep it from moving.

Treating Fractures, Dislocations, Sprains, and Strains

The objective when treating a suspected fracture, sprain, or strain is to immobilize the injury and the joints immediately above and below the injury site.

Because it is difficult to distinguish among fractures, sprains, or strains, if uncertain of the type of injury, treat the injury as a fracture.

Fractures

A fracture is a complete break, a chip, or a crack in a bone. There are several types of fractures.

- A **closed fracture** is a broken bone with no associated wound. First aid treatment for closed fractures may require only splinting.
- An **open fracture** is a broken bone that goes through the skin.

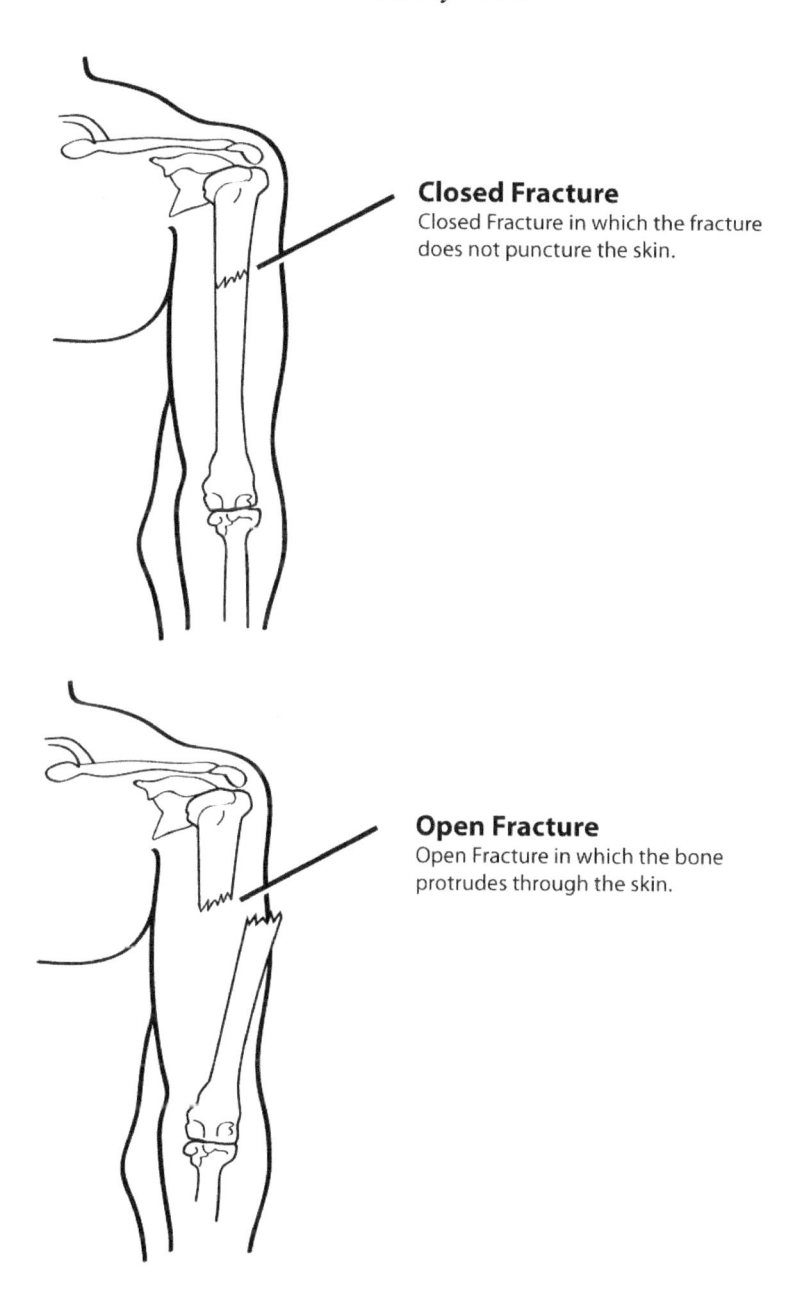

Closed Fracture
Closed Fracture in which the fracture does not puncture the skin.

Open Fracture
Open Fracture in which the bone protrudes through the skin.

Open fractures are more dangerous than closed fractures because they pose a significant risk of severe bleeding and infection. Therefore, they are a higher priority and need to be checked more frequently.

When treating an open fracture:
- Do not draw the exposed bone ends back into the tissue.
- Do not irrigate the wound.

You should:
- Cover the wound with a sterile dressing
- Splint the fracture without disturbing the wound
- Place a moist 4 by 4-inch dressing over the bone end to keep it from drying out

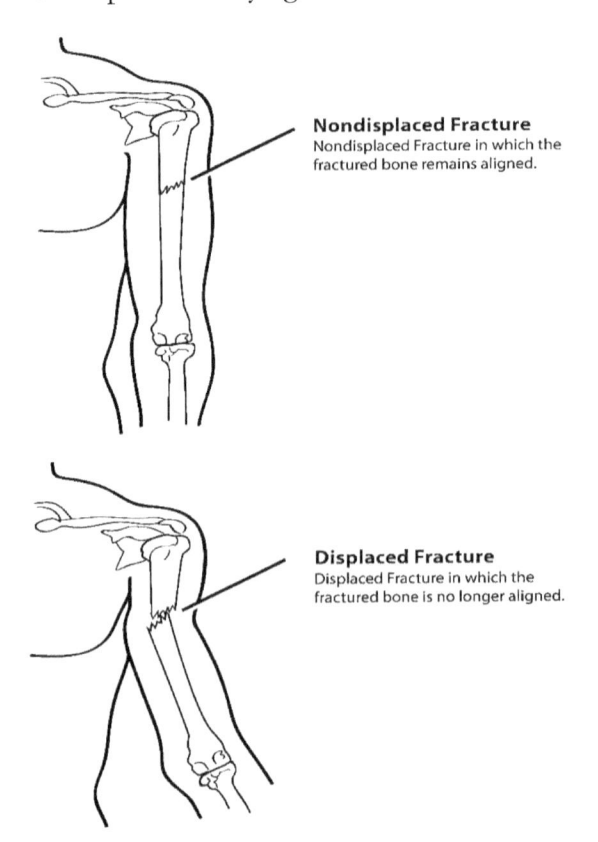

Nondisplaced Fracture
Nondisplaced Fracture in which the fractured bone remains aligned.

Displaced Fracture
Displaced Fracture in which the fractured bone is no longer aligned.

If the limb is angled, then there is a **Displaced Fracture**. Displaced fractures may be described by the degree of displacement of the bone fragments.

Non-Displaced Fractures are difficult to identify, with the main signs being pain and swelling. You should treat a suspected fracture as a displaced fracture until professional treatment is available.

Dislocations

Dislocations are another common injury in emergencies.

A dislocation is an injury to the ligaments around a joint that is so severe that it permits a separation of the bone from its normal position in a joint.

The signs of a dislocation are similar to those of a fracture, and a suspected dislocation should be treated like a fracture.

If dislocation is suspected, be sure to assess PMS (Pulse, Movement, and Sensation) in the affected limb before and after splinting/immobilization.

You should not try to relocate a suspected dislocation. You should immobilize the joint until professional medical help is available.

Sprains and Strains

A sprain involves a stretching or tearing of ligaments at a joint and is usually caused by stretching or extending the joint beyond its normal limits.

A sprain is considered a partial dislocation, although the bone either remains in place or is able to fall back into place after the injury.

The most common signs of a sprain are:

- Tenderness at the site of the injury
- Swelling and/or bruising
- Restricted use or loss of use

The signs of a sprain are similar to those of a non-displaced fracture. Therefore, you should not try to treat the injury other than by immobilization and elevation.

A strain involves a stretching and/or tearing of muscles or tendons. Strains most often involve the muscles in the neck, back, thigh, or calf.

In some cases, strains may be difficult to distinguish from sprains or fractures. Whether an injury is a strain, sprain, or fracture, treat the injury as if it is a fracture.

Splinting

Splinting is the most common procedure for immobilizing an injury.

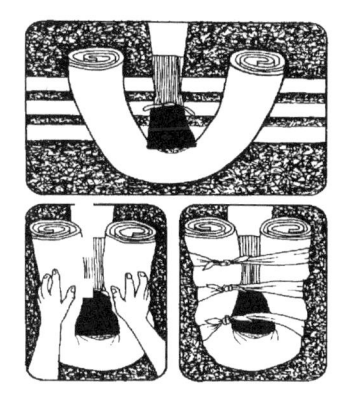

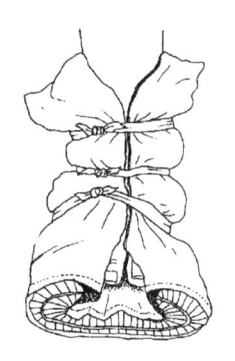

Cardboard is the material typically used for makeshift splints but a variety of materials can be used, including:

- Soft materials. Towels, blankets, or pillows, tied with bandaging materials or soft cloths
- Rigid materials. A board, metal strip, folded magazine or newspaper, or other rigid item

Anatomical splints may also be created by securing a fractured bone to an adjacent non fractured bone. Anatomical splints are usually reserved for fingers and toes, but, in an emergency, legs may also be splinted together.

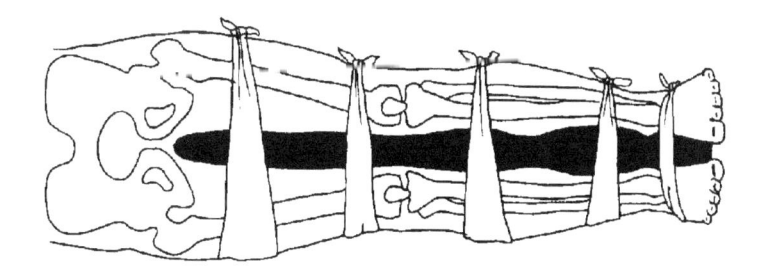

Soft materials should be used to fill the gap between the splinting material and the body part.

With this type of injury, there will be swelling. Remove restrictive clothing, shoes, and jewelry when necessary to prevent these items from acting as unintended tourniquets.

Nasal Injuries

Bleeding from the nose can have several causes:
- Blunt force trauma to the nose
- Skull fracture
- Non trauma-related conditions such as sinus infections, high blood pressure, and bleeding disorders

A large blood loss from a nosebleed can lead to shock.

Actual blood loss may not be evident because the victim will swallow some amount of blood. Those who have swallowed large amounts of blood may become nauseated and vomit.

To control nasal bleeding:
- Pinch the nostrils together
- Put pressure on the upper lip just under the nose

While treating for nosebleeds, you should:
- Have the victim sit with the head slightly forward so that blood trickling down the throat will not be breathed into the lungs. Do not put the head back.
- Ensure that the victim's airway remains open
- Keep the victim quiet. Anxiety will increase blood flow.

Survival Family Basics

Head tilted forward

Squeeze firmly above nostrils

Child sits in adults lap

© Kids Health Info
RCH, Melbourne

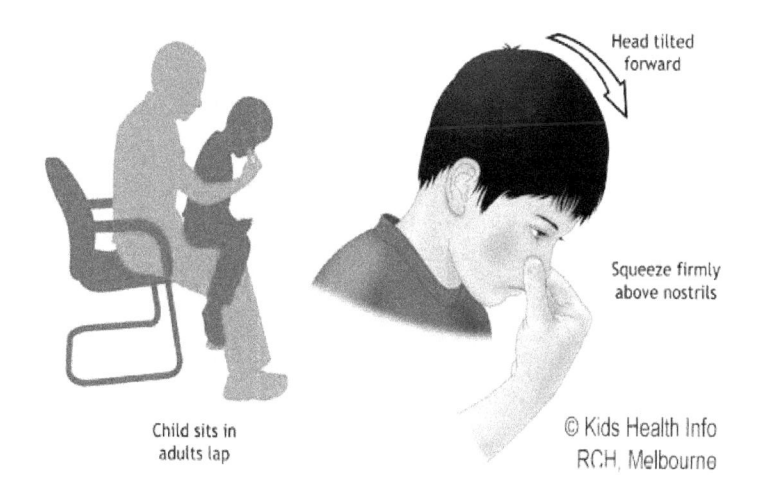

Bites and Stings

In a disaster environment, everything is shaken from normalcy, including insects and animals. In times of chaos, insect bites and stings may be more common than is typical as these creatures, like people, are under additional stress.

When conducting a head-to-toe assessment, you should look for signs of insect bites and stings. The specific symptoms vary depending on the type of creature, but, generally, bites and stings will be accompanied by redness and itching, tingling or burning at the site of the injury, and often a welt on the skin at the site.

Treatment for insect bites and stings follows these steps:

1. Remove the stinger if still present by scraping the edge of a credit card or other stiff, straight-edged object across the stinger. Do not use tweezers; these may squeeze the venom sac and increase the amount of venom released.

2. Wash the site thoroughly with soap and water.
3. Place ice (wrapped in a washcloth) on the site of the sting for 10 minutes and then off for 10 minutes. Repeat this process.

You may help the victim take his or her own allergy medicine (Benadryl, etc.), but rescuers should not dispense medications unless licensed to do so.

Allergic Reactions & Anaphylaxis

The greatest concern with any insect bite or sting is a severe allergic reaction, or anaphylaxis. Anaphylaxis occurs when an allergic reaction becomes so severe that the victim's airway is compromised.

If you suspect anaphylaxis:
1. Check airway and breathing.
2. Calm the individual.
3. Remove constrictive clothing and jewelry as the body often swells in response to the allergen.
4. If possible, find and help administer a victim's Epi-pen. Many severe allergy sufferers carry one at all times.
5. DO NOT administer medicine aside from the Epi-pen. This includes pain relievers, allergy medicine, etc.
6. Watch for signs of shock and treat appropriately.

Treating Cold-Related Injuries

Cold-related injuries include:

Hypothermia, which is a condition that occurs when the body temperature drops below normal; and frostbite, which occurs when extreme cold shuts down blood flow to extremities causing the tissue to die.

Hypothermia

Hypothermia may be caused by exposure to cold air or water or by inadequate food combined with inadequate clothing and/or heat, especially in older people.
The primary signs and symptoms of hypothermia are:
- A body temperature of 95 degrees F (37 degrees C) or lower
- Redness or blueness of the skin
- Numbness accompanied by shivering

In later stages, hypothermia will be accompanied by:
- Slurred speech
- Unpredictable behavior
- Listlessness

Because hypothermia can set in within only a few minutes, you should treat victims who have been rescued from cold air or water environments.
- Remove wet clothing.
- Wrap the victim in a blanket or sleeping bag and cover the head and neck.
- Protect the victim against the weather.
- Provide warm, sweet drinks and food to conscious victims. Do not offer alcohol.

- Do not attempt to use massage to warm affected body parts.
- If the victim is conscious, place him or her in a warm bath.
- Place an unconscious victim in the recovery position:

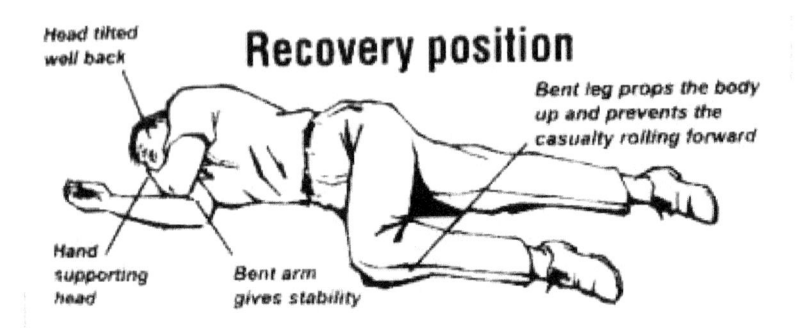

Recovery position

Head tilted well back
Hand supporting head
Bent arm gives stability
Bent leg props the body up and prevents the casualty rolling forward

  o Place the victim's arm that is nearest to you at a right angle against the ground, with the palm facing up.
  o Move the victim's other arm across his or her chest and neck, with the back of the victim's hand resting against his or her cheek.
  o Grab a hold of the knee furthest from you and pull it up until the knee is bent and the foot is flat on the floor.
  o Pull the knee toward you and over the victim's body while holding the victim's hand in place against his or her cheek.
  o Position the victim's leg at a right angle against the floor so that the victim is lying on his or her side.

Do not to allow the victim to walk around even when he or she appears to be fully recovered. If the victim must be moved outdoors, cover the head and face.

Frostbite

A person's blood vessels constrict in cold weather in an effort to preserve body heat. In extreme cold, the body will further constrict blood vessels in the extremities in an effort to shunt blood toward the core organs (heart, lungs, intestines, etc.).

The combination of inadequate circulation and extreme temperatures will cause tissue in these extremities to freeze, and in some cases, tissue death will result.

Frostbite is most common in the hands, nose, ears, and feet.

There are several key signs and symptoms of frostbite:
- Skin discoloration (red, white, purple, black)
- Burning or tingling sensation, at times not localized to the injury site
- Partial or complete numbness

A patient suffering from frostbite must be warmed slowly! Thawing the frozen extremity too rapidly can cause chilled blood to flow to the heart, shocking and potentially stopping it.

- Immerse injured area in warm (NOT hot) water, approximately 107 degrees F.
- Do NOT allow the body part to re-freeze as this will exacerbate the injury.
- Do NOT attempt to use massage to warm body parts.

Wrap affected body parts in dry, sterile dressing. Again, it is vital this task be completed carefully. Frostbite results in the formation of ice crystals in the tissue; rubbing could potentially cause a great deal of damage!

Treating Heat-Related Injuries

There are several types of heat-related injuries that you may encounter in a disaster scenario:

- Heat cramps are muscle spasms brought on by over-exertion in extreme heat.
- Heat exhaustion occurs when an individual exercises or works in extreme heat, resulting in loss of body fluids through heavy sweating. Blood flow to the skin increases, causing blood flow to decrease to the vital organs. This results in a mild form of shock.
- Heat stroke is life-threatening. The victim's temperature control system shuts down, and body temperature can rise so high that brain damage and death may result.

Heat cramps

Heat cramps are typically a sign that the body is in need of water. Place the individual in a cooled area or out of the direct sun. Encourage the victim to drink water or drinks containing electrolytes. Electrolyte drinks could also be added to your emergency first aid kit for these situations.

Heat Exhaustion

The symptoms of heat exhaustion are:

- Cool, moist, pale, or flushed skin
- Heavy sweating
- Headache
- Nausea or vomiting
- Dizziness
- Exhaustion

A patient suffering heat exhaustion will have a near normal body temperature. If left untreated, heat exhaustion will develop into heat stroke.

Heat Stroke

Heat stroke is characterized by some or all of the following symptoms:
- Hot, red skin
- Lack of perspiration
- Changes in consciousness (fainting especially)
- Rapid, weak pulse and rapid, shallow breathing

In a heat stroke victim, body temperature can be very high — as high as 105° F. If an individual suffering from heat stroke is not treated, death can result.

Handling the Dead

While this is certainly something I hope you will never have to deal with, I would be remiss to leave this section out.

No matter how much preparation and training you have, in a major disaster there are bound to be some who don't survive.

If you encounter these poor souls the two important steps in caring for the deceased during an emergency are safe and dignified management of the body and identification.

During a large scale disaster the initial response is hectic and chaotic.

Local government officials will have identified, in governmental plans formed prior to a disaster, where mortuary site locations will be in the event of one. These locations are refrigerated areas where temperatures can be kept at 35 to 40 degrees Fahrenheit.

Recovery of the deceased is often handled by local emergency responders but, it may take quite some time for them to get there.

It is not recommended that you attempt cremation or burial, and burials in mass graves should only be handled by disaster response officials.

While the full psychological impact of dealing with the disaster, the injured, and the dead may be delayed due to the phases of survival or even shock, it is a stressful and deeply saddening time for all involved, and everyone deals with this stress differently.

Survival Family Basics

That said, it is important to stay calm. If necessary, take time to calm those around you, and gently separate individuals who won't be calmed and who pose a threat to themselves or others from the area you are working in.

In a disaster situation where there are known to be multiple deaths and/or injuries. It is important to provide as much documentation as possible for each body.

Write as much information as you can identify the deceased. If possible use a permanent marker and try to ensure the information will be visible on the body and protected from the environment. Sealable plastic bags with sheet of paper inside work well.

- Write the deceased name.
- Date of Birth (if known)
- Location found
- Time of death or time body found
- Identifying marks, tattoos, scars
- Any other information that you feel may be useful.

If there are items at the scene you feel have been separated from the deceased such as jewelry, wallet, shoes, etc....place those in a bag and secure to the body.

Duct tape works well for this.

Handle the body with dignity and wrap in a sheet or plastic and place in a body bag. A tarp will work well if a body bag is not available.

Secure with rope or duct tape.

At this point, you may once again, using a permanent marker, write the deceased's name on the wrapping with the location they were found.

Please keep in mind, it is not body remains that cause an epidemic after a disaster. Disease spreads from the fecal matter that has left the body and is normally released following death.

Make sure the area where the death occurred is cleaned if time permits. All cleaning items should be placed in a trash bag and disposed of. Most experts recommend burying the trash bag and debris if they cannot be burned. If items are buried, dig the hole deep enough to keep animals from recovering the items.

After completing the steps necessary to care for the dead, wash your hands thoroughly and dispose of any contaminated items in a trash bag and secure it well.

Take a deep breath and move on.

Conclusion

I hope this book was able to help give you a practical working knowledge of emergency first aid and survival medicine and the basic first aid supplies needed to survive a disaster or to provide initial first aid to the injured.

As you begin prep your emergency medical kit, you will open up to a new world of security and possibility. Remember to prepare as a family and with an eye toward your unique lifestyle. Always have a kit for all aspects of your life.

Walk through your home and begin gathering items and making list of what you will need in the way of first aid supplies and survival medicine to prep for an emergency.

Speak to your neighborhood health food store and request of herbs that would be beneficial for your medical kit.

As with any hands on techniques, it is always best to practice to get good at performing first aid. The Red Cross offers formal training in first aid and CPR becoming certified can never hurt.

Remember, this guide can be the first item in your emergency first aid kit. Share this with your friends and co- workers.

Finally, if you enjoyed this book, please take the time to share your thoughts and post a review on Amazon. It'd be greatly appreciated!

Thank you and good luck!

Macenzie

Check out these other *Survival Family Basics* Titles...

http://www.amazon.com/dp/B00HG7Y4YS

http://www.amazon.com/dp/B00HYQ55W6

http://www.amazon.com/dp/B00J1V939S

http://www.amazon.com/dp/B00JXU7OBG

http://www.amazon.com/dp/B00K00DMQE

References

www.fema.gov

www.cdc.gov

www.homelandsecurity.gov

www.nationalweatherservice.gov

CPSIA information can be obtained
at www.ICGtesting.com
Printed in the USA
LVHW080246100322
713102LV00013B/577